LifeGuide®FAMILY Bible Studies

for Parents and Kids to Do Together

MW00397101

Wisdom Workshop

18 Studies on Wise Sayings from Proverbs

With Notes for Parents

Darrel A. Trulson

General Editor
James C. Galvin, Ed.D.

InterVarsity Press
Downers Grove, Illinois 60515, USA

Crossway Books
Leicester, UK

InterVarsity Press
P.O. Box 1400, Downers Grove, IL 60515, USA

Crossway Books
38 De Montfort Street, Leicester LE1 7GP, UK

InterVarsity Press®, U.S.A., is the book-publishing division of InterVarsity Christian Fellowship®, a student movement active on campus at hundreds of universities, colleges and schools of nursing in the United States of America, and a member movement of the International Fellowship of Evangelical Students. For information about local and regional activities, write Public Relations Dept., InterVarsity Christian Fellowship, 6400 Schroeder Rd., P.O. Box 7895, Madison, WI 53707-7895.

LifeGuide® is a registered trademark of InterVarsity Christian Fellowship.

All Scripture quotations are from the International Children's Bible, New Century Version, *copyright © 1986, 1988, 1994 by Word Publishing, Dallas, Texas 75039. Used by permission.*

This book was developed exclusively for InterVarsity Press by The Livingstone Corporation. James C. Galvin, Daryl J. Lucas and Linda R. Joiner, project staff.

Cover photograph: Michael Goss

Activities: Deborah Peska-Keiser

USA ISBN 0-8308-1117-6
UK ISBN 1-85684-130-8

Printed in the United States of America ∞

26	25	24	23	22	21	20	19	18	17	16	15	14	13	12	11	10	9	8	7	6	5	4	3	2	1
17	16	15	14	13	12	11	10	09	08	07	06	05	04	03	02	01	00	99	98	97	96	95			

CONTENTS

Welcome to LifeGuide® Family Bible Studies

If you have ever wondered how to make Bible study fun for kids, you will be delighted with this series of study guides. It provides an easy way to study the Bible with a young child or all together as a family. LifeGuide® Family Bible Studies were created especially for families with children ages 4-12. The simple, friendly format makes it easy for adults and children to finish together in just fifteen minutes a day. The material is undated so you can work through the guide at your own pace and according to your family's schedule.

Getting the Most from LifeGuide® Family Bible Studies

Understanding the format used in this series allows you to adapt each lesson to the needs of your family. Each lesson includes a passage from the Bible to read together, questions to discuss, fun activities and a prayer. You can spend more time on some sections and less on others, depending on the age and needs of your child.

Opening. When you sit down together, you need some way to focus your child's attention. The introductory paragraphs start with the child's frame of reference and leads him or her to the truth presented in the Bible passage. Often, the opening includes a question to ask your child or family so that you can find out more about what they are thinking. The opening also creates interest in the Bible verses for that lesson. If your child can read, have him or her read both the opening and the Bible text.

Bible Reading. The translation used in these study guides is the *International Children's Bible.* Having the text reprinted in the study guides makes it easy to use, and also allows children to use highlighters and colored pencils in their study of the Scriptures without fear of ruining a Bible. If you prefer, you can easily use other Bibles in conjunction with the lesson. Either way, the Bible reading usually generates questions.

Discussion Questions. Each lesson includes several questions to discuss to deepen your understanding of the passage. Some of the questions will require your child to look for the answers in the Bible reading. Others will help your child to think about how the truths apply to life.

✎More difficult questions for older children are marked with a pencil.

Activity. Each study guide contains a variety of fun paper and pencil activities such as simple crossword puzzles, mazes and decoding games. These activities can help motivate kids to complete the lesson each day. If you are sharing one study guide with several children, you can take turns letting each child complete the puzzle for the day.

Prayer. The main point of the lesson is also expressed in the prayer that you and your child can pray together. You can add more to each prayer as appropriate. But your child may not want to stop there.

Bonus. We have also included an active learning experience for a longer session when you have time and your child wants to do more. Or, you may want to save it for another day. The bonus activity provides additional reinforcement for the main point of the lesson.

Notes to Parents. You will find notes conveniently placed in the margins of each lesson rather than in a separate leader's guide. These notes provide practical help as you study the Bible together.

Studying the Bible with Children

You will find it useful to keep developmental differences in mind as you study the Bible together. After all, children are not miniature adults, and they would not learn well from Bible study approaches suitable for adults. The following chart illustrates some of the characteristics of children at different ages and relates them to Bible study. Which have you noticed in your own child?

Ages	Characteristics of Children	Implications for Bible Study
4-5 early childhood	In general, children this age: • learn by asking questions • usually have many fears • sometimes confuse make-believe with reality • have a growing sense of right and wrong • have a relatively short attention span (5-10 minutes)	As you teach your child: • allow them to ask questions, and answer them patiently • discuss God's protection • don't be surprised if Bible stories get mixed up with pretend stories • distinguish between right and wrong • don't expect to finish each lesson in one sitting
6-8 middle childhood	• are emergent readers; some are fluent readers • think concretely and literally; abstractions tend to be difficult • are able to memorize information easily • thrive on approval from their parents	• use this as an opportunity to practice reading skills • discuss the here and now, avoiding abstractions • make a game out of memorizing a few short verses from a study guide • praise and encourage as much as possible
9-11 later childhood	• are beginning to reason more logically • want to be independent learners • eagerly enter into competitive activities • have many questions about Christianity	• use the questions marked with a pencil, which are more challenging to answer • let your child set the pace and read as you facilitate • try not to have a winner and loser of the Bible study • help your child find answers to his or her questions in the Bible

With so many differences between older and younger children, you will have to adapt some lessons and skip certain activities. You may want to encourage the older children to help the younger ones. Think of these lessons as a helpful guide. Answering your child's questions may ultimately be more important than finishing a lesson. The following guidelines will help you adapt the lessons to meet the needs of children of different ages.

Using These Studies as a Family

You can use these studies to guide your family devotions. If you do, the biggest challenge will be keeping the attention and interest of both younger and older children at the same time. One useful technique for leading the discussion is to ask the question, then allow the children to answer one at a time, starting with the youngest and moving in order to the oldest. This way the younger children have a chance to talk, and the older children have a chance to add their answers. Don't let one child be critical of another child's answer. Parents can join in the fun, too. Your children will be interested in the personal applications that you see in the lesson.

You may have to change some of the wording in the lessons. When using the prayer as a family, change the *me* and *my* to *us* and *our*. Also, you may not want to do the puzzle as a group. Above all, keep it fun. Try to end with a snack or treat of some kind. You may find that your family wants to work through the entire series.

Using These Studies with a Younger Child

Younger children have boundless energy and short attention spans. Keep each lesson short and sweet. You may not be able to finish every lesson in one sitting; if so, just finish up the next day. Make use of the bonus activities at the end because these are more active in nature.

In general, don't use the questions marked with a pencil.

Some of the puzzles are designed to appeal to younger children, and some to older children. Feel free to skip the puzzles that seem too difficult.

Allow your child to ask questions at any point in the lesson. Sometimes the questions may seem endless, but that is a sign that your child is learning. Praise and encourage your child as much as possible during the study.

If your child cannot read, read the prayer one phrase at a time and have the child repeat it after you. Encourage your child to express his or her feelings to God in prayer, and also to make requests to his or her Heavenly Father.

If your child is an emergent reader, make the Bible study a fun experience by letting him or her circle important words or use a highlighter (just like Mom and Dad). Colored pens and pencils can add excitement to the lesson. Make Bible study an adventure.

Using These Studies with an Older Child

Older children don't want to be treated like little kids. They will quickly spot the parts of each lesson intended for younger children. If this happens, don't argue. Simply let them know that they will be treated differently, that they don't have to do all the parts of every lesson, and that this study should be very *easy* for them to complete.

In general, skip the bonus activities, because these are primarily for younger children. You can let your child choose whether or not to complete the puzzle in each lesson. Some of them will be far too easy, and some will be a challenge. The discussion questions marked with a pencil are more difficult and are for older children. Don't skip these. You may want to keep a concordance and Bible dictionary handy for questions that come up along the way.

Older children can be challenged to begin a personal devotional life. If appropriate for your child, consider letting him or her work alone on the study as a step toward developing a personal quiet time. Discuss the lesson with your child after he or she has answered all the questions.

The LifeGuide® Family Bible Studies

The entire series includes eight different study guides. Each study guide contains 18 lessons on a particular topic. Start with the topics that would be most interesting to your family.

Super Bible Heroes. The Bible is full of people who did great things, heroic things. But they really aren't very much bigger or stronger or braver than you. Reading their stories, you'll see how God can help you do what seems impossible on your own.

Grown Up on the Inside. Just as food, exercise and rest help us grow up on the outside, the Bible shows us how to grow up on the inside. It shows us how to practice being loyal, humble, honest, respectful and caring—everything that God knows will make us happy and healthy.

Fruit-Filled. Everybody has a favorite: blueberry Pop-Tarts, apple pie, Jell-O with bananas in it. The Bible tells us how we can be filled with God's favorite fruits: love, joy, peace, patience, kindness, goodness, faithfulness, gentleness and self-control.

Good Choice, Bad Choice. Every day we make choices: Will I watch TV or play outside after supper? What will I do when someone makes me mad? The Bible shows us how God helped other people make decisions—and how he will help us.

Jesus Loves Me. Jesus is the friend who never disappoints us or moves to another city. He is the friend who always understands our problems, who always has time to listen and help. The Bible shows us many ways Jesus loves us and helps us see his care in the things that happen to us every day.

The Friendship Factory. Friends make life fun. They help us learn, grow and know God better. And what the Bible says about friendship can help us be better friends to the people we know.

Wisdom Workshop. King Solomon wanted to be wise. So he asked God for wisdom. In the book of Proverbs he tells what God helped him learn about wisdom—and what you can learn too.

God's Great Invention. God made comets and colors and kangaroos. But his greatest invention is people—people like you. The Bible shows how God made you different from everyone else, with gifts and talents to make your own special mark on his world.

No matter which study guide you begin with, you will be introducing your child to the exciting challenge of studying God's Word and planting the seeds for a lifetime habit of personal Bible study.

James C. Galvin
General Editor

1

Allow time for your child to answer.

Eager to Learn

Do you like to learn new things? Sometimes learning is hard work, but it is also very interesting. At home, at school and at church we learn new things every day.

The Bible tells us that learning is very important. The book of Proverbs tells us that the person who is eager to learn from others and from God is a wise person. But it also says that people who do not want to learn get into a lot of trouble. We can find out more about being wise by studying Proverbs.

Bible Reading

[8]A wise person is praised. But a stupid person is not respected. (Proverbs 12:8)

[12]Remember what you are taught. And listen carefully to words of knowledge. (Proverbs 23:12)

[10]A wise man will learn more from a warning than a foolish person will learn from 100 lashings. (Proverbs 17:10)

Discussion

1. What are you interested in learning?

2. What do people often say about someone who is always ready to learn (Proverbs 12:8)?

3. What are some good ways to help yourself remember what others teach you (Proverbs 23:12)?

4. Proverbs 17:10 tells us that a wise person can learn from a warning. When have you learned not to do something by being warned?

When have you had to learn by being disciplined?

Which did you like better? Why?

5. Why does God want us to be wise?

✎6. How can God's Word help you to become a wise person?

✎7. How can you be a wiser person tomorrow than you are today?

Activity

R	E	M	E	M	B	E	R	W	N	F	N
E	D	W	L	O	O	C	L	E	A	R	N
S	U	W	O	R	D	S	I	Y	N	O	P
P	W	I	S	E	I	O	S	G	S	D	R
E	H	L	O	P	P	N	T	R	L	L	A
C	R	L	C	M	U	T	E	U	N	A	I
T	A	U	G	H	T	P	N	O	T	A	S
F	O	O	L	I	S	H	E	N	L	Y	E

Find the following words from the Scripture reading in the diagram above. Words may appear vertically, horizontally or diagonally.

WISE	PRAISE	RESPECT	LISTEN	WILL	FOOLISH	REMEMBER
PERSON	STUPID	TAUGHT	WORDS	MAN	LEARN	NOT

Prayer

Dear God,
Thank you for giving me so many ways to learn every day. Help me always to be eager to learn. Thank you for your Word, which tells me how to become wise. Thank you for giving us the book of Proverbs in the Bible.
In Jesus' name, amen.

Bonus

Through nature we can learn a lot about God and the world he created. Take a walk outside and go on a nature hunt. Look for something new or interesting you can bring back to your room and put on display. It could be a fascinating rock or an oddly shaped stick. No matter what you find, use it to remind and teach you that we always have more to learn and that God is always eager to teach us.

· · · · · · · · · · · · · · · ·

2

For a good illustration on the power of words, you and your child can read James 3:1-12 together.

Watch What You Say

Have you ever stopped to think that your tongue can hurt people? The Bible calls it a sharp sword because it is very powerful. With your tongue you can make someone sad, or you can say something good and make them happy.

The book of Proverbs reminds us to be careful about what we say. Listen to what the Bible says about kind words and mean words and what they can do.

Bible Reading

[21]A wise person is known for his understanding. He wins people to his side with pleasant words. (Proverbs 16:21)

[24]Pleasant words are like a honeycomb. They make a person happy and healthy. (Proverbs 16:24)

[18]Careless words stab like a sword. But wise words bring healing. (Proverbs 12:18)

Discussion

1. What good things can come from pleasant words (Proverbs 16:21, 24)?

2. What is the difference between careless words and wise words (Proverbs 12:18)?

3. Have you ever been hurt by words someone said to you? What happened?

4. What are some of the pleasant words you especially like to have someone say to you?

5. Why is it good to think about our words before we say them?

✎6. What are some good things you can say to a friend or family member?

✎7. Who do you know who speaks kindly to others and always seems to make others happy?

What can you learn from watching this person?

7. Help your child talk about someone he or she knows who has good relationship skills and sets a godly example. Children often respond positively to such a person but may not have thought about the specifics of this person's behavior.

Activity

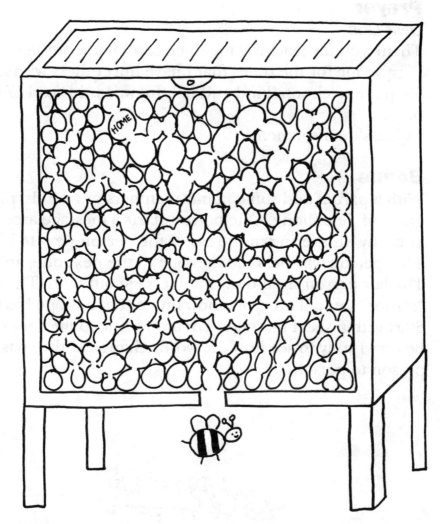

The Bible reading says, "Pleasant words are like a honeycomb." Help the bee find its way home through this honeycomb.

Prayer

Dear God,
Thank you for teaching me to be careful about the words I say.
Forgive me for the times that I have hurt others with my words.
Help me to choose kind and helpful words instead of mean ones.
In Jesus' name, amen.

Bonus

When the game is over, help your child to see that the misunderstandings might not be funny if the message being passed was something that really mattered. Help him or her to think back on what Proverbs says about careless versus wise words.

With a parent and some family members or friends, play a game of Telephone. One person starts a message around the circle by whispering in the ear of the person next to him or her. That person whispers the message to the next one, and so on. The last person should say the message out loud. Then the "starter" can tell everyone how much the message has changed. Start with a short message. Then try some longer ones. It can be very funny to see how the words change as they pass from person to person.

③

Don't Get Angry Quickly

Have you ever seen funny pictures or cartoons of people who were so angry they had steam coming out their ears? Maybe they even looked ready to explode! Pictures like these make us laugh, but real people with bad tempers are not funny.

Proverbs teaches us that blowing up in anger is not good for us or the people around us. God's way is to control our tempers and to be careful what we do with our anger.

For additional passages on anger, see Proverbs 16:32; 19:11, 12, 19; 20:2; 21:14, 19.

Bible Reading

¹⁸A person who quickly gets angry causes trouble. But a person who controls his temper stops a quarrel. (Proverbs 15:18)

²⁴Don't make friends with someone who easily gets angry. Don't spend time with someone who has a bad temper. ²⁵If you do, you may learn to be like him. Then you will be in real danger. (Proverbs 22:24-25)

Discussion

1. What trouble might you cause if you let your anger out without thinking?

2. Why should we stay away from someone who gets angry easily (Proverbs 22:24-25)?

3. What causes you to get angry?

4. What are some ways you can control your temper?

5. What good things can come from controlling your anger?

✎6. How might you learn to be like people with bad habits just by being around them?

✎7. When *should* you do something about your anger after you have thought about it?

Activity

But a

_ _ _ _ _ _ who

_ _ _ _ _ _ _ _

his _ _ _ _ _ _

stops a

_ _ _ _ _ _ .

Start at the arrow and write every other letter in the blanks. You will complete the sentence and discover a key phrase from the Bible reading.

Prayer

Dear God,
Please forgive me for the times I get angry quickly. Help me to do better at controlling my anger. Thank you that I can talk to you whenever I am angry.
In Jesus' name, amen.

Bonus

Play a pretending game with a parent. Have your parent pretend to be another child who takes your favorite toy away from you. Show two different ways you could react: first, show what you might do if you lost your temper; then, show a better way to deal with your anger.

In preparation for the next study you may want to photocopy the puzzle so that it can be cut out.

4

Allow time for your child to answer.

Respect for God

Who is a person you look up to, someone you want to please? Those feelings are all part of what we call *respect*. We respect someone who knows more than we do and can teach us many things.

As Christians, we respect God most of all. He knows *everything* and is able to help us with all our needs.

Bible Reading

[27]Whoever respects the Lord will have a long life. But an evil person will have his life cut short. (Proverbs 10:27)

[26]A person who respects the Lord will have security. And his children will be protected. [27]Respect for the Lord gives life. It is like a fountain of water that can save people from death. (Proverbs 14:26-27)

Discussion

1. What kind of person does not respect God (Proverbs 10:27)?

2. What kind of blessings does the Lord promise to give those who respect him (Proverbs 10:27 and 14:26-27)?

3. How does it help us to feel safe when we know and respect the Lord of heaven and earth?

4. How can respect for the Lord save people from death (Proverbs 14:27)?

5. How can we show our respect for God by the way we live?

✎6. Why would a person who fears God tend to live longer than someone who doesn't?

✎7. Where can you learn more about what it means to respect God?

4. Respect for God can protect us from physical death. But it also saves us from the spiritual death of separation from God for eternity. Respect for God includes realizing our sinfulness before his perfection and believing in the sacrifice of his Son for our salvation.

5. Help your child to make applications regarding how he or she thinks and behaves in daily life.

6. Although we shouldn't encourage children to think that all believers live longer than other people, respect for God clearly promotes healthy, life-giving habits and discourages the self-destructive patterns of sin. Depending on your child's age, you might want to discuss ignoring instructions from a parent or teacher that were meant to protect them from harm (such as running across a street) and taking drugs or abusing the body in other ways.

7. Some of the answers to explore with your child might include the Bible, older Christians, the church and parents.

Activity

Use the pieces to complete the puzzle. Hint: You will find part of the Bible reading. Don't peek! Permission to photocopy this page granted by InterVarsity Press.

Prayer

Dear God,
Thank you for all the blessings that come from respecting you.
Help me to think about you and want to please you more and
more.
In Jesus' name, amen.

Bonus

Think of the people who are older and wiser than you. Who do
you respect? Ask a parent to write down a list. Tell what it is you
respect about each person. Together, thank God for these
special people in your life and ask him to make you more like
them each day.

People You Respect	Why You Respect Them

5

Glad for Discipline

If appropriate, discuss with your child the last time he or she was disciplined by you. Ask what he or she learned from that situation. Explain that you discipline because God has commanded you to do it, and that you love them and want them to grow up to do what is right.

No one likes to be told no. We would all like to eat all the candy we want, or stay awake as late as we like. However, we do not always know what is good for us. That is why God gave us parents. They teach us what is right and wrong.

When we sin, our parents must discipline us, because that is what God has told them to do. It's not that our parents want to make us sad, but they want us to grow up to be wise and to follow God.

Bible Reading

[1]A wise son takes his father's advice. But a person who makes fun of wisdom won't listen to correction. (Proverbs 13:1)

[24]If a person does not punish his children, he does not love them. But the person who loves his children is careful to correct them. (Proverbs 13:24)

[15]Every child is full of foolishness. But punishment can get rid of it. (Proverbs 22:15)

Discussion

1. How does disciplining a child show love (Proverbs 13:24)?

2. Why is it wise to take your father's or mother's advice (Proverbs 13:1)?

3. Helping your child to focus on lessons already learned will set a positive tone for the discussion.

3. What are some foolish things that you used to want to do?

4. Tell your child about a bad habit that you are trying to break. This will show your child that he or she is not alone in the learning process, that you understand the struggle this can be and that you can be a positive example to your family in trying to change.

4. What are some behaviors you are trying to correct now?

5. Why do your parents discipline you?

6. How do you feel when someone makes fun of people who do what's right?

7. Your child can think of what it will be like when he or she becomes a parent.

7. What do you think is difficult about disciplining children?

Activity

CVIEAD   __ __ __ __ | __ __

NSO   __ | __ __

FAECULR   __ __ | __ __ __ __

OSRNEP   __ __ | __ __ __

VLOSE   __ __ __ | __ __

ANC   __ __ __

ENTLSI   __ __ __ | __ __

Unscramble the letters on the left to reveal words from the Bible reading. When the letters are unscrambled, a word will appear in the column down the middle that describes what parents are told to do for their children.

Prayer

Dear Lord,
Thank you for giving me a parent who loves me enough to discipline me. Help me to listen to correction and learn not to do what's foolish.
In Jesus' name, amen.

Bonus

Choose a doll or stuffed animal for your parent and one for yourself. Then play a game of pretend. When the dolls (or animals) do something wrong that needs correction, you and your parent can talk about the best way to discipline them for their own good.

Being Humble

"I can run faster than you can." "Oh yeah, well I have more toys than you do." "Big deal, my toys are nicer." Does this sound familiar? People of all ages like to brag about what they can do or what they own. However, this is not the way the Bible teaches us to act. When we are proud, we think only of ourselves, but when we are humble, we help the people around us.

God wants us to know how he feels about proud people. Even though they think they are very important, God knows different. He is watching out for the people they ignore.

Bible Reading

[4]Respecting the Lord and not being proud will bring you wealth, honor and life. (Proverbs 22:4)

[6]Don't brag to the king. Don't act as if you are a great man. [7]It is better for him to promote you to a higher job than to give you a less important position. (Proverbs 25:6-7)

[34]The Lord laughs at those who laugh at him. But he is kind to those who are not proud. (Proverbs 3:34)

Discussion

1. How do you feel when someone brags in front of you? Why?

2. What good things often happen to people who are *not* proud (Proverbs 22:4)?

3. Why could a person end up feeling silly if he or she bragged to the king (Proverbs 25:6-7)?

4. Why doesn't God like people to be proud?

5. Why do you think God blesses humble people (Proverbs 3:34)?

✎6. Why is it sometimes hard not to brag about things we have or things we can do?

✎7. What are some ways you can tell that someone is humble?

2. This is not a guarantee that humble people will enjoy great success but a statement of what often happens when people have a humble attitude about the choices they make. Humble people avoid many of the traps that lead to poverty (such as conspicuous spending), humiliation (such as foolish boasts) and even death (such as insistence on keeping a destructive habit). Humility, in other words, protects us from many of life's dangers, and that often does lead to wealth, honor and life.

5. You may want to explain that humble people simply admit their proper place before God. It's not that they think of themselves as more lowly than they are. Proud people, by contrast, close their eyes to the many ways God has enabled them. There's no way God can help such people until they become humble.

Activity

t	1. To crash or roll down	____ umble
st	2. To foul up	____ umble
f	3. To trip	____ ____ umble
m	4. To break	____ ____ umble
cr	5. To mutter	____ umble
j	6. A mess	____ umble

Use the definitions provided to reveal the words that rhyme with *humble*.
Use the letter combinations to the left to help you.

Prayer

Dear God,
Forgive me for the times that I have bragged and made others feel bad. Help me to remember how you feel about proud people. Help me to become a more humble person.
In Jesus' name, amen.

Bonus

When your family is around the supper table or gathered in the living room, play a game with your family called "I'm Happy for You." You can go first. Think about the person on your right: What new skill did that person learn lately, or what new thing did that person get that he or she really wanted? Tell the family by saying, "I'm happy for you that . . ." Then the next person talks about the one to his or her right, until everyone has had a turn. After the game, talk about how it felt to have someone be happy for you without having to brag about it first.

Being Honest

Allow time for your child to answer.

Pete did not know what he should do. The teacher had found a broken window near the playground where he and his friends were playing. Now the teacher was asking, "How did that window get broken?" It would be easy for Pete to say, "I don't know." But really, Pete knew he broke the window with his baseball. What should Pete say to his teacher?

Lying may offer a quick solution to a problem, but it is the wrong solution. The Lord wants us to be honest so we can be a witness to the world about the truth of God.

Bible Reading

[22]People want others to be loyal. So it is better to be poor than to be a liar. (Proverbs 19:22)

[13]Kings are pleased with those who speak honest words. They value a person who speaks the truth. (Proverbs 16:13)

[19]Truth will last forever. But lies last only a moment. (Proverbs 12:19)

Discussion

1. What should you do if someone offers you a lot of money to tell a lie (Proverbs 19:22)?

2. Why do you think a king or ruler would like to have honest people around (Proverbs 16:13)?

✎3. Why do you think truth lasts longer than lies (Proverbs 12:19)?

4. Would you trust someone if they had lied to you or cheated you in the past? Why or why not?

5. Why should we keep from telling lies, even if we think we'll never be caught?

6. When was a time you found it difficult to be honest? Why?

✎7. When have you been glad to have an honest friend? Why?

2. Explain to your child that people who have power over others have a lot of responsibility. Many people want to tell them how to use their power. If people are selfish and willing to lie, they can cause trouble for rulers. So rulers need to have people around them who will tell them the truth.

3. Reflect with your child that, even if a lie accomplishes what we want now, it is always possible that the people we lied to will find out the truth sometime later. Truth, however, doesn't change, so we don't have to worry about what people will find out.

5. Many children will think it's bad to lie because they might be punished. This is normal. Help them see that it's wrong because God wants us to tell the truth.

Activity

Connect the dots from 1 to 20 and from A to P to discover what kings are pleased with.

Prayer

Dear God,

Thank you for teaching me that truth is important. Please help me to be honest in all I do. When I am tempted to lie, help me to be strong and not to sin. Help me to tell the truth all the time. In Jesus' name, amen.

Bonus

Choose a family member to be blindfolded and then place an object somewhere in the room. Now appoint two other people to coach the blindfolded person to pick up the object. (Invite a friend over if you don't have enough family members.) The trick is, only one of the "coaches" will be telling the truth. The other coach will be leading the person in the wrong direction. The blindfolded person will have to listen carefully and decide whom to listen to and what direction to take. The coaches cannot touch the person. They can only persuade him or her with their voices. Then discuss the difference between truth and lies.

Allow time for your child to answer.

8

Laziness

What is your favorite kind of work? Most of us have some work that we like to do and other work that we dislike. When we don't like a chore we have to do, we sometimes try to put it off, or we try to get someone else to do it for us. At those times we are being lazy.

God wants us to see that it is not smart to allow ourselves to be lazy. Most of God's other creatures would not be able to live if they didn't do their work. In the same way, we are only hurting ourselves if we don't learn how to do our work whether or not we "feel like it." The book of Proverbs uses an example from nature to teach us about hard work.

Bible Reading

[6]Go watch the ants, you lazy person. Watch what they do and be wise. [7]Ants have no commander. They have no leader or ruler. [8]But they store up food in the summer. They gather their supplies at harvest. [9]How long will you lie there, you lazy person? When will you get up from sleeping? [10]You sleep a little; you take a nap. You fold your hands and rest. [11]So you will be as poor as if you had been robbed. You will have as little as if you had been held up. (Proverbs 6:6-11)

Discussion

1. Why do ants work hard in the summer (Proverbs 6:8)?

2. Children may not relate to this example because they do not see their physical needs being met directly by their own labor. You might share some of the things that are expected of you if you are to earn a living. You might also share some work experiences from your childhood that helped you develop good work habits for the future.

2. Why might you end up poor if you are never willing to work?

3. What kinds of work are you tempted to put off or try to get out of doing?

4. "Lazy" is a label that children are all too ready to put on one another. You can help your child to understand that it is too simplistic to assume that people who are not obviously working are therefore being lazy. A person might not know how to do a task, he or she might feel ill, have a disability or be thinking up a way to do something (planning) before doing it.

4. What is the difference between being lazy and resting when you are tired?

5. Is it good to work hard? Why?

✎6. Why do people often need someone standing over them (like a commander) before they will work hard or work together?

7. By helping your child reflect on accomplishments of which he or she is rightly proud, you can reinforce some of the satisfying aspects of work.

✎7. When have you felt especially good about some hard work you have done?

Activity

The book of Proverbs tells us to be like the ant. Find the two ants that are exactly alike.

Prayer

Dear Lord Jesus,
Thank you for giving us the example of the ants, who work so hard to make sure they have what they need to live. Help me not to be lazy when there is work to be done.
Amen.

Bonus

With a parent, go to the library or get an encyclopedia or colorful book about insects and look up *ants*. See what interesting facts you can learn about ants and how they work. Talk together about ways you both could work hard like the ants.

9

Allow time for your child to answer.

Depend on God

What can you now do by yourself that you used to have to ask someone for help with? It is a good feeling when we learn to do things on our own. But if we start to think that we are so smart or so strong that we don't even need God, then we are headed for trouble.

God doesn't want anyone, even grownups, to feel that they don't need him anymore. And he says that if we depend on him, he will make sure that we succeed.

Bible Reading

⁵Trust the Lord with all your heart. Don't depend on your own understanding. ⁶Remember the Lord in everything you do. And he will give you success. (Proverbs 3:5-6)

³Depend on the Lord in whatever you do. Then your plans will succeed. (Proverbs 16:3)

³⁰There is no wisdom, understanding or advice that can succeed against the Lord. (Proverbs 21:30)

Discussion

1. What will the Lord do for us if we remember that we need him (Proverbs 3:5-6)?

2. What else do people depend on instead of God (Proverbs 3:5-6)?

3. Who is smart enough to go against God and win (Proverbs 21:30)?

4. With some prompting, your child will probably be able to identify times, either in the present or from the recent past, when things seemed to be going wrong. At those times, children and adults alike wonder if God's promises of success are true. Encourage your child to persevere at such times. Also, help him or her to understand that the world's definition of success may not be the same as God's.

4. When are some times you find it hard to trust the Lord?

5. Help your child to see that godly character is more important to God than wealth or prestige. The world around us may not always consider Christians "successful," but in God's eyes those who depend on him *are* successful.

5. What do you think God means when he promises us success?

✎6. What does it mean to remember the Lord in everything you do?

✎7. What plan or goal are you trusting God with right now?

Activity

$$\underline{}\;\underline{}\;\underline{}\;\underline{}\;\underline{}$$
6   14   12   9   6   **the**

___ ___ ___ ___   ___ ___ ___ ___   **all**
2 13 14 7   8 5 6 4

___ ___ ___ ___ ___ ___ ___ ___ ___ .
10 13 12 14 3 11 1 14 6

To discover a key phrase from Proverbs, solve the problems below to find the missing letters.

L	W	H	T	Y	R	E
1+1=	2+6=	3+1=	4+2=	7+3=	11+3=	6+5=

U	O	H	I	D	A	S
10+2=	8+5=	2+1=	3+2=	4+3=	1+0=	6+3=

Prayer

Dear Lord,
Thank you that I am growing up and learning to do many things by myself. Thank you that even when I am grown up I can still depend on you. Thank you for your love and care for me.
In Jesus' name, amen.

Bonus

To get an idea of what it feels like to depend on someone else, try this game with a parent or other family member. First, you should choose a book or other medium-sized object that you will carry with both hands. Then walk through the house together for 5 to 10 minutes. (It may be hard to remember to use both hands. If you forget and reach for something with one hand, remind yourself and go back to carrying your object.) You will have to depend on the other person if you need to reach anything, turn pages in a book, or eat while your hands are busy. Talk about the funny things that happen and all of the ways you need your own hands throughout the day.

10

Listening to Good Advice

Allow time for your child to answer.

Timmy is having a problem with another boy in his class who is threatening him. Timmy feels like going to the teacher or his mom for help, but he is afraid. He asks his big brother what to do. Together they tell their mother and get Timmy some help.

Are you the kind of person who asks for advice first, or the kind who likes to try things yourself? It's wise to ask for help when you need to make a decision but don't know what to do. We shouldn't be shy to ask for help when we need it. Good sources for this help include our parents, teachers, pastors, and especially the Bible. When we ask other people for advice, it helps us to make wise decisions.

Bible Reading

[22]Plans fail without good advice. But plans succeed when you get advice from many others. (Proverbs 15:22)

[18]Get advice if you want your plans to work. If you go to war, get the advice of others. (Proverbs 20:18)

[17]Pay attention and listen to what wise people say. Remember what I am teaching you. (Proverbs 22:17)

Discussion

1. Do you find it hard or easy to ask advice from others? Why?

2. What should we do if we want our plans to work (Proverbs 15:22 and 20:18)?

3. What kind of people should we ask for advice (Proverbs 22:17)?

4. Tell about your own experience as well. Adults are often more aware than children of missed opportunities.

4. When have you wished you had paid better attention to what someone told you?

5. This is a good opportunity to assure your child that he or she can always come to you for advice with any problem in life.

5. Why should you ask other people for advice?

✎6. What are some examples of good advice that you have received from the Bible?

✎7. Who is someone that you have recently asked for advice? Why did you choose this person?

Activity

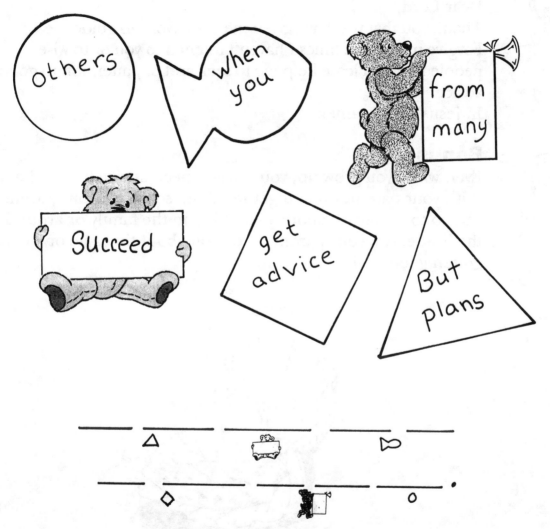

To find a truth about good advice, rearrange the words according to the symbols.

Prayer

Dear Lord,

Thank you that you have given me your Word to guide me. Forgive me for the times I haven't listened to you or to wise people I know. Please help me to seek and pay attention to good advice.

In Jesus' name, amen.

Bonus

Even when you grow up, you will still need advice from others. With your parent, think together about someone your parent can go to for advice about something in the family or around the house. Ask your parent to tell you about times he or she has gotten good advice.

Using Money Wisely

Allow time for your child to answer.

About how much money do you have? Perhaps you keep it in a piggy bank. Maybe you even have a bank account. What do you like to use your money to buy?

We all like to have money to buy the things we need and want. Most of us wish we had more money. We try to think of ways to earn it. But the Bible reminds us that money is not always a good thing. It can become so important to us that it controls us. It can also be used to help or to hurt other people. For Christians, what we do with our money is more important than how much we have.

Bible Reading

²⁸Those who trust in riches will be ruined. But a good person will be as healthy as a green leaf. (Proverbs 11:28)

¹⁷Being kind to the poor is like lending to the Lord. The Lord will reward you for what you have done. (Proverbs 19:17)

⁸It is better to be poor and do what is right than to be wealthy and be unfair. (Proverbs 16:8)

Discussion

1. Why is it unwise to trust in riches (Proverbs 11:28)?

2. The Bible tells us that God cares about those who don't have their needs met in this world. We have the opportunity, as his servants, to be part of the solution. When we do this, it is as if we were doing it for God himself. Jesus' words are very similar in Matthew 25:31-40. If your child seems interested, you could read that passage together at the end of this lesson.

2. Why is it good for us to lend to the poor (Proverbs 19:17)?

3. What is more important—how much money we have or how we treat other people (Proverbs 16:8)?

✎4. Should we treat rich people like they are more important than everyone else? Why or why not?

5. Discuss with your child other riches which God gives to us that are not material in nature.

5. Can money buy you everything you need? Why or why not?

6. How does God want us to use our money?

✎7. Does being wealthy always mean having money? Explain your answer.

Activity

To reveal a picture, color in only the areas that contain a letter. Hint: Proverbs says that we will be like these.

Prayer

Dear Lord,
Thank you for the money you have given to me and my family.
Help me to remember that all good gifts come from you. Help me
to always be ready to use some of my money to help other people.
In Jesus' name, amen.

Bonus

Ask your parent to help you choose a place to give some of your
own money. It might be a friend who needs something, a
missionary who brings God's Word to children who don't know
him, or an organization that helps find food, clothing and
shelter for needy people. When you send or take your gift, be
sure to pray for the people who will receive it.

12

Learning to Be a Good Worker

What is a job you do especially well? It feels good to be told we are good workers. Becoming a good worker means trying hard, even when the job you're doing is not your favorite. It means staying with a job until it is done—and done right!

There are many proverbs in the Bible about working hard. It is important for us to be good workers so we can take good care of ourselves and our families. This is a way we serve God.

Allow time for your child to answer. If your child can't readily think of an example, mention a task for which you can readily and honestly praise him or her.

Bible Reading

^{24}Hard workers will become leaders. But those who are lazy will be slaves. (Proverbs 12:24)

^{23}Those who work hard make a profit. But those who only talk will be poor. (Proverbs 14:23)

^{13}If you love sleep, you will be poor. If you stay awake, you will have plenty of food. (Proverbs 20:13)

Discussion

1. Who will be the leaders and who will be the slaves (Proverbs 12:24)?

2. What do you have to do to make money (Proverbs 14:23)?

3. If sleep is always more important to a person than work, what could happen to that person (Proverbs 20:13)?

4. Who do you know who is a good worker? Why do you think so?

5. What are some ways that you can become a better worker?

✎6. Why is it sometimes hard to finish a job and do it well?

7. There are many work metaphors in Scripture for our service to God. Jesus called his disciples to become "fishers of men." He also sought "laborers for the harvest." If your child is interested, you might read Matthew 4:17-25 or Matthew 9:35—10:1 together.

✎7. What does it mean to work for God?

Activity

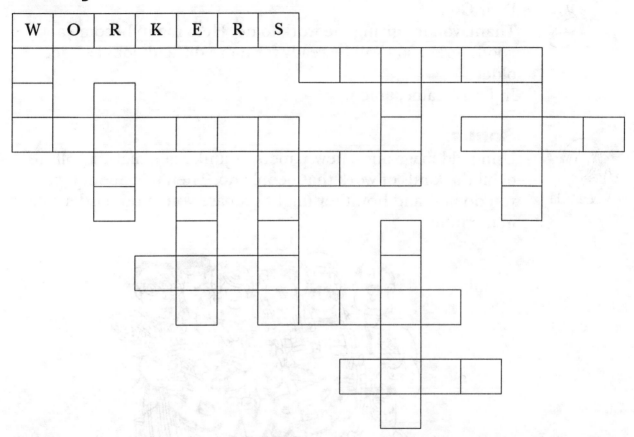

The words listed all appear in the Bible reading. Use them to complete the cross-word. Hint: Start with the longest words first.

4 Letters
hard   poor
will   stay
lazy   food
only   love

5 Letters
those
sleep

6 Letters
slaves
profit
plenty

7 Letters
workers
leaders

Prayer

Dear God,

Thank you for giving me work to do. Help me to become a good worker so I will be ready for more difficult jobs as I get older.

In Jesus' name, amen.

Bonus

Using old magazines, newspapers or junk mail, make a collage of all the kinds of work that people do. Then talk about jobs you do now and how they might prepare you to do harder jobs in the future.

13

Don't Be Jealous

What is something that a friend or brother or sister has that you really wish you had? It is not wrong to know what you want. But if you think too much about the other person having something you want, you may become jealous. Envy and jealousy are feelings that can eat away at us on the inside and make us unhappy. The Bible teaches us to watch out for envy and jealousy.

Bible Reading

[30]Peace of mind means a healthy body. But jealousy will rot your bones. (Proverbs 14:30)

[17]Don't envy sinners. But always respect the Lord. [18]If you do, you will have hope for the future. Your wishes will come true. (Proverbs 23:17-18)

[1]Don't envy evil people. Don't try to be friends with them. [2]In their minds they plan cruel things. And they always talk about making trouble. (Proverbs 24:1-2)

Discussion

1. What does jealousy feel like on the inside (Proverbs 14:30)?

2. Why is it dangerous to envy evil people (Proverbs 23:17 and 24:1)?

3. What will happen if we respect God instead of envying evil people (Proverbs 23:17-18)?

4. Who are you tempted to envy, and why?

5. The way we get what we want reveals much about our true motives. Envy and jealousy will lead us to use selfish and destructive means. If we are being selfish or rude, we need to stop and ask whether we are having a problem with envy or jealousy.

5. Why is it important to pay attention to *how* we get the things we want?

✎6. When have you felt miserable because you were so jealous?

What did you do?

7. Second Timothy 2:22 addresses the avoidance of sins such as envy. You and your child might want to read and discuss this verse together.

✎7. What are some ways you can keep envy out of your heart?

Activity

hope for the future	talk about making trouble	wishes will come true	envy sinners
a healthy body	but always respect	be jealous	plan cruel things
make friends with evil people	envy evil people	peace of mind	the Lord

Cross out the squares that contain the answers to the following two statements. The two squares left form a key expression from today's reading.

1. According to the Bible reading, what six things are we not to do?

2. Proverbs states that we will have these four things if our hearts are free from jealousy.

Prayer

Dear Lord,
Forgive me for the times that I envy what other people have. Help me not to be a jealous person. Help me to learn that the best way to be happy is to follow you.
In Jesus' name, amen.

Bonus

One good way to feel less jealous of what other people have is to remember to be thankful for what you have. Take a large sheet of paper and some markers or crayons. Think about all you have that makes you feel thankful. Then see how many of those things you can draw on the paper. When you are finished, count them and talk about what you drew. You might like to ask an adult to label the pictures to help you remember all your blessings.

14

Allow time for your
child to answer.

God Is in Control

What do you want to be when you grow up? At first Liz wanted
to be a firefighter. But then she started school and decided to
be a teacher instead. Then she learned more about her dad's
job and changed her mind. Now she wants to be an engineer
like he is.

It is fun to think about the future and plan for what we would
like to happen. But sometimes things don't go exactly the way
we planned. It can feel like everything is going wrong. At times
like that, it is good to know that God is in control.

Bible Reading

[4]The Lord makes everything work the way he wants it. He even
has a day of disaster for evil people. (Proverbs 16:4)

[9]A person may think up plans. But the Lord decides what he
will do. (Proverbs 16:9)

[24]The Lord decides what a person does. So no one can
understand what his life is all about. (Proverbs 20:24)

Discussion

1. What is good about making plans?

2. What is bad about making plans?

3. If your plans are different from God's plan, what will happen (Proverbs 16:9)?

✎4. Should we stop making plans because only God knows what will really happen?

5. What should we do instead of worrying about the future?

✎6. How can it help us to know that God will punish evil people who don't repent and turn to him?

✎7. Why do you think God doesn't tell us everything he knows about the future?

4. This sort of question is likely to occur to children. Help them to understand that we must continue to live our lives using the Scriptures as guides for our goals and decisions. However, it can actually be comforting to rest in the sovereignty of God at times when our wisdom and resources are limited.

5. Because worry is not a foreign experience to children, they can understand that taking excessive responsibility for what happens to us can cause us to worry more than we would need to. As you discuss these proverbs, and as circumstances occur in your child's life, help him or her to turn to prayer when he or she feels worried.

6. The people who live their lives exploiting others will also have to answer to God. If there is someone who is currently in the role of frustrating good plans in your child's life, help him or her to see that God knows what is happening and that he will take care of it, both now and in the future. God does grieve for the lost, but he also keeps accounts and will ensure justice.

Activity

ever	pple	se	im
land	ator	on	not

1. apple

2. whatever

3. landlord

4. impersonator

5. does not

6. these

7. decides on

<table>
<tr><td>_____</td><td>_____</td><td>_____</td><td>_____</td></tr>
<tr><td>6</td><td>3</td><td>7</td><td>2</td></tr>
</table>

<table>
<tr><td>_____</td><td>_____</td><td>_____ .</td></tr>
<tr><td>1</td><td>4</td><td>5</td></tr>
</table>

Cross out the letters in the numbered words that match the letters in the boxes. Copy the smaller words that remain on the lines that have the same number below. You will find a message from Proverbs.

Prayer

Dear Lord,
Thank you for being so wise and powerful that you know everything about our lives. When I don't understand all that is happening to me, help me to trust you and to turn to you in prayer.
In Jesus' name, amen.

Bonus

It can be fun to plan ahead and then look back to see how your plans turned out. Before you go to bed tonight, have a parent help you write down everything you *think* you will do tomorrow. At the end of the day, get out your list and see what happened. Did you do most of the things you planned? Did you do some other things you didn't plan?

Making Good Friends

Who are some of your good friends? Good friends are wonderful! We tell them our secrets. We play and share our lives with them. Friends are important because they can help us become better people.

    The Bible tells us to be careful about the friends we choose, because friends will influence us to become like them. The people we choose to be our friends need to be good people so that we can follow their example.

Allow time for your child to answer.

Ideally, we would like our children's "best" friends to hold values similar to ours. If some of your child's friends are not from Christian homes, you can help him or her to appreciate what they have in common but to hold onto the beliefs that the friends do not share.

Bible Reading

[20]Whoever spends time with wise people will become wise. But whoever makes friends with fools will suffer. (Proverbs 13:20)

    [9]Whoever forgives someone's sin makes a friend. But the one who tells about the sin breaks up friendships. (Proverbs 17:9)

    [24]Don't make friends with someone who easily gets angry. Don't spend time with someone who has a bad temper. (Proverbs 22:24)

Discussion

1. Why would a foolish person not be a good friend (Proverbs 13:20)?

1. In the Bible a fool is any person who lacks a desire to do right.

2. Why would forgiving someone make him or her a friend (Proverbs 17:9)?

3. Why is it a bad idea to spend time with someone who has a bad temper (Proverbs 22:24)?

4. How have some of your friends helped you become a better person?

5. What kinds of traits make a person a good friend?

5. Encourage your child to describe the qualities of such a friend.

6. This might be an opportunity, especially with older children, to talk about peer pressure and the desire to "fit in." These factors can cause anyone to abandon values and behaviors that really are important to them, as Proverbs recognizes.

✎6. Why do you think people change when they are around someone who is a bad influence?

✎7. Why does someone who tells others about someone else's sins make a bad friend (Proverbs 17:9)?

Activity

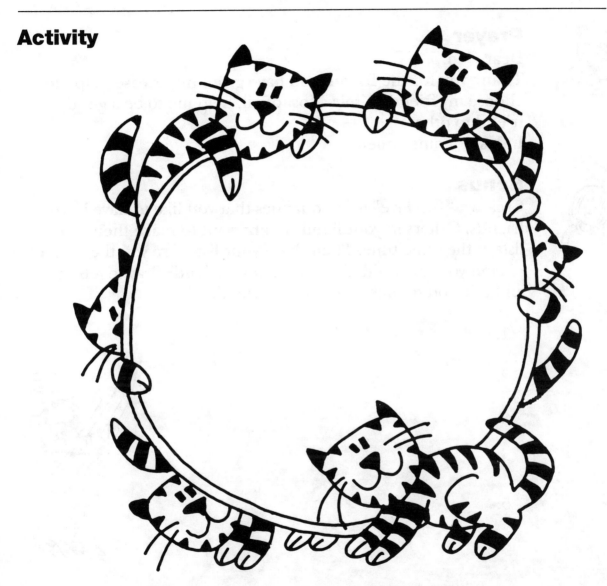

Fill this picture frame with pictures of your good friends.

Prayer

Dear God,

Thank you for the friends you have given me. Please help me to choose my friends wisely. Most of all, help me to be a good friend to others.

In Jesus' name, amen.

Bonus

Create a "Top Five" list of qualities that you like to have in your friends. Others in your family might want to make their own lists at the same time. Then share your lists. Are you the kind of person you say you'd like to have for a friend? Pray together and ask God to make you a good friend.

1.

2.

3.

4.

5.

16

Obeying Your Parents

Allow time for your child to answer.

Who is a favorite teacher you have had at school or at church? There is someone you probably don't think of as a teacher, but he or she has been teaching you longer than anyone—your parent!

In Proverbs, many of the verses start out, "My son . . ." The wise truths that Proverbs tells us are very much like the lessons we learn from our parents. It is a good idea to take advantage of the built-in teachers we have in our own homes!

Bible Reading

[1]A wise son makes his father happy. But a foolish son makes his mother sad. (Proverbs 10:1)

[7]The son who obeys what he has been taught shows he is smart. But the son who makes friends with those who have no self-control disgraces his father. (Proverbs 28:7)

[20]My son, keep your father's commands. Don't forget your mother's teaching. [21]Remember their words forever. Let it be as if they were tied around your neck. [22]They will guide you when you walk. They will guard you while you sleep. They will speak to you when you are awake. [23]Their commands are like a lamp. Their teaching is like a light. And the correction that comes

from them helps you have life. (Proverbs 6:20-23)

Discussion

1. What is the difference between children who make their parents happy and those who make them sad (Proverbs 10:1)?

2. What is one good way to show that you are smart (Proverbs 28:7)?

3. What good comes from listening to the wise teachings of parents (Proverbs 6:20-23)?

4. When do you find it most difficult to obey your parents? Why?

5. What are some ways that you can help yourself *remember* the things your parents teach you?

6. Some possibilities include: what to do about a mean kid, how to build or make something, how to play a game and so on.

7. Try to listen non-judgmentally to your child's answer. You may learn about a lesson that he or she is struggling with or discover a teaching that especially hits home. You can also contribute here regarding your own parents.

✎6. When was a time when your parents' advice helped you make a wise choice?

✎7. When you are a parent, what is one of the first lessons you will want your children to learn?

Activity

A̸ B C̸ D E̸ F G H I J̸ K L M N

MA __ ES

__ ELPS

SA __

__ EEN

FR __ ENDS

__ O

__ IGHT

LI __ E

__ UARD

LA __ P

Use the letters above to complete the words that are listed. Letters that you won't use are already crossed off. Hint: All the words above appear in the Bible reading.

Prayer

Dear Lord Jesus,
Thank you for giving me parents to teach me about life. Help me to respect my parents and listen to their teaching.
Amen.

Bonus

Play a game to test your memory. Ask your parent to tell you one good piece of advice he or she would like you to remember. Ask questions if you don't understand exactly what it means. Then say it over two or three times. Finally, put a Band-Aid on your finger as a "reminder." Every time you see the Band-Aid, remind yourself of the advice. Tomorrow, sit down with your parent and see if you can still explain the good advice you received.

17

Be a Good Neighbor

How many of your neighbors can you name?

Allow time for your child to answer.

Usually, we can't choose our neighbors the way we do our friends. But neighbors can become good friends. They can help us in many ways because they live close by. We can help them if we are good neighbors. The Bible teaches us about being good neighbors.

Bible Reading

[28]If you have what your neighbor asks for, don't say to him, "Come back later. I will give it to you tomorrow." [29]Don't make plans to hurt your neighbor. He lives nearby and trusts you. (Proverbs 3:28-29)

[10]Don't forget your friend or your father's friend. Don't always go to your brother for help when trouble comes. A neighbor close by is better than a brother far away. (Proverbs 27:10)

[14]Don't greet your neighbor loudly early in the morning. He will think of it as a curse. (Proverbs 27:14)

Discussion

1. Why is it good to cooperate with our neighbors (Proverbs 3:28-29)?

2. Why is it sometimes better to ask a neighbor for help than a relative (Proverbs 27:10)?

3. If you have moved recently or are not acquainted with many of your neighbors, help your child recall an instance from the past, or relate one from your own experiences pre-children.

3. How have neighbors been a help to you or your family?

4. What things do we do that our neighbors don't like (Proverbs 27:14)?

5. What can you do this week to be a good neighbor?

✎6. What sorts of things should we do if we want to keep our friends?

✎7. How can we help our neighbors when they have troubles?

Activity

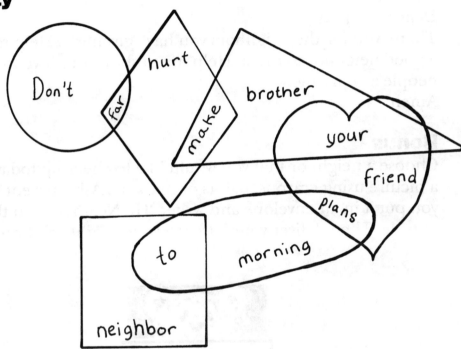

You will uncover a message to you from Proverbs by answering the questions below and filling in the answer in the space above the question.

What word is in the circle but not in the diamond?	What word is in the diamond and in the triangle?	What word is in the heart and the oval but not in the triangle?	What word is in the square and the oval?	What word is not in the circle or the triangle but is in the diamond?	What word is in the heart and the triangle but not in the oval?	What word is not in the oval but is in the square?

76

Prayer

Dear Lord Jesus,

Thank you for the neighbors you have given me. Help me to be a good neighbor to them. Help me to show your love to the people around me.

Amen.

Bonus

Choose a neighbor that you would like to cheer up today. Draw a picture using crayons, paints or markers. Ask a parent to help you put it in an envelope and write, "Hi, Neighbor" on the outside. Then deliver your letter to your neighbor's house.

18

How to Be Happy

What could someone do for you that would make you really happy?

Many times, we think in terms of things that happen to us to make us happy. We receive a nice present or a special visitor or get to do something we really want to do. All of these things feel very good. But did you know that there are things *you* can do that will make you a happier person? The Bible tells us about some of these things. They are surprising because many of them have to do with thinking about other people instead of ourselves.

Your child's answer might be outlandish, like a request for a large sum of money or an expensive toy. In that case, try to take a lighthearted approach, emphasizing that this was a hypothetical question, not an offer! Then ask again for something more realistic.

Bible Reading

¹³Happy is the person who finds wisdom. And happy is the person who gets understanding. (Proverbs 3:13)

²¹It is a sin to hate your neighbor. But being kind to the needy brings happiness. (Proverbs 14:21)

²⁴Pleasant words are like a honeycomb. They make a person happy and healthy. (Proverbs 16:24)

Discussion

1. How can finding wisdom help to make us happy (Proverbs 3:13)?

1. You may need to give some illustrations so your child can see that a wise person is able to avoid harmful influences and seek out positive ones. Also, wisdom gives us a better perspective on our current circumstances.

2. If your child is interested, you could read Acts 20:35, where Paul passes along Jesus' teaching that it is more blessed to give than to receive.

6. All of the proverbs listed here suggest things that are within our control. We tend to think of happiness as something that *happens* to us, but the Bible encourages us to establish some habits that will actually lead to happiness.

2. Why do you think it could make *you* happy to be kind to someone in need (Proverbs 14:21)?

3. How do pleasant words spoken to you help you feel happy (Proverbs 16:24)?

How do pleasant words spoken *by* you make others happy?

4. Why is it hard to be happy when you are feeling hateful?

5. What could you do this week that would make you a happier person?

✎6. What kinds of things can you do to help make sure that you will be happy?

✎7. Where can you find the kind of wisdom that will make your life happier?

Activity

😊 is the 🎩on who finds wisdom. And 😊 is the 🎩on who gets under🦋ing.

It is a sin to hate 🐛r neighbor. But 🐝ing kind 2 the 📖dy b👀 😊ness.

Pleas🐜 words are like a honey 🍯. Th🖌 make a 🎩on 😊 and healthy.

This is the Bible reading with a few changes. Without peeking, try to figure out what the symbols mean.

Prayer

Dear Lord,
Thank you for teaching me ways that I can live that will help my life to be happy. Help me to be kind, to speak pleasant words and to look for wisdom. Thank you for loving me and wanting me to be happy.
In Jesus' name, amen.

Bonus

Make a list of pleasant words you can use around your house. Find some ways to use these words today!

Pleasant Words